73

Keep Your Little Lights Alive

☙

by John-Francis Quiñonez

Write Bloody Publishing

writebloody.com

First edition.
ISBN: 978-1949342451

Cover Design by Zoe Norvell
Interior Layout by Angelo Maneage
Edited by Wess Mongo Jolley
Proofread by Wess Mongo Jolley
Author Photo by Kristen Haines

Type set in Bergamo.

Printed in the USA

Write Bloody Publishing
Los Angeles, CA

Support Independent Presses
writebloody.com

KEEP YOUR LITTLE LIGHTS ALIVE

RE: THE 9TH WAVE (B)

"Come on, Baby
Oh, come on
Come on, Darling"

LET ME STEAL THIS MOMENT FROM YOU NOW

I know that we will never get it back!
these many miracle worlds in the broth
may soothe our cold & feeling — thought I'd share
this morning light holds up my shirts, warms me
had to survive the years, arise so sharp
we could cut each other up, hard edges
I'm scared — there's danger in an honest town
look up and the flakes fall like blanket-stars
each grows wider to hide the dreaming hours
Look around! Maybe just the two of us!
each zipper zips and button fastens, yes
we fall apart when our knots come undone

we fall together like leaves returning
the track starts & rings through the branches (click)!

I beg us — look in awe, quick!
de-gnarl your fingers, my love!
my own spread & check for yours
labors for hope, tills water
desperate ache — beg for soft
settle for tiny embers
guard my ears, whispers hurt me
neighbors 'neath the earth bellow
this song tickles my arches
Feel this with me! Listen!
none of this was made for us
and yet we wake to these gifts

Quick! What can I plug into?
I have something to show you!

(click) !

RE: HOUNDS OF LOVE (A)

"Tell me,
we both matter,
don't we?"

Re: Running Up That Hill (A Deal with God)

Christmas in the Desert
is a thing God only considers in jest —
candy lights strewn for no evergreen
just chapped bramble, spikes against the soft holly.

This cacti in false starlight
is Drag, but only in jest
and there is no God in such a thing.

I never wear tights, even when I want to,
for occasions or always,
because my leg hair stands the
netting some inch above my actual leg.

And so there I stand again
with two trunks dressed for no holiday,
again and again,
before I never leave the house lit up
again and again —
a congregation to no passage.

Churches are tragic/funny to me
built into sharp towers —
bristle to the palm of comfort
God's house with no room for them, even.
Nothing built in honor
that says *reach your hand out and rest here, child* —
just Holy left *looking in*.
The word only reaches wanting ears
through walls and brick and window
& no wonder why no one seems to answer our song in full.
Hear only what they want to —
The palatable. Loudest among them. Gagged or cackled.

Kate Bush sings to me several rooms over
& I hear what I think is

> *If I only could,*
> *I'd make a deal with God,*
>   *And get them to swallow places*

& bless.
All Queer bodies exist in hymn, Lord.
Glow like fairy lights in the desert —
Soft rejoice amidst the violence.
Just short of a prayer at arms length.

And so
I pray as the Nair chars up my thigh —
a high forest in spots of crimson.
The chorus goes

   If I only could,
    I'd make a deal with God,
     And get them to swap our places

but I do not want that.
Not like this.

I get so drunk to leave the house in a dress —
Wet as God's mouth. Legs smooth as a kept joke.
It snows in Phoenix, and I wonder who is laughing.
I work in silence — hang up the last
few rows of lights up the pecan tree
staple by staple and I swear

the branches
they were all bleeding.

It's in the Trees, It's Coming

it follows   urges doubt   to blossom   in the dark

afraid   of the street   what y'all think of this

it's coming   *from me*   through the trees   the sound

hard rattles —   *help me!*   *help me someone!*   *help me please!*

take my shoes off   try to breathe, halt   halt, the water

is all that can be found   save my hands beneath my

heart — it beats so fast   *so* fast   so fast   so fast, so fast   so

ashamed of all/nothing real to point to —

                just can't deal with this   afraid to be here

among your watch   and arms   I sink standing

        it surrounds me, holds me down   it's coming

don't help me, *help me* —   tell me   what's *for me?*

I don't know what's   for me   I trust you to

        tell me   if the answer is   *nothing*

I trust you *not* to tell me if the answer is   *all of it*

Dress A

boy with the threat of being found out.
What could you still do? Thirsty?   No remedy.
   What do you cup your hands for, then?
                                       Salt, butter.
How far to push till you finger the spine —
                      Should this dry hurt?
                            Can I wash with this wet?

Dress a fish to be caught for the many.
Dress a boy so they can eat & still   they   cease   in the eyes.

All this time out at sea — so thirsty

                         living on salt, butter.
Butter for the knuckles, deep in the soft
fish — would it hurt
              if you saw how beautiful I dressed you, in thyme?
Would your
    salt-water dress
          run clear from you in time,
or is this the bright of you? Is that your aroma?

Salt, lemon.   so thirsty!
So thirsty?
      Then drink, then
           curl your fingers together
                    into a cup
                     and drink, then.
Not for the many,
        but to butter this hurt
           & forget this craving —
left buried
      in your soft.

Amphibious or Undone

I do not know what of this has been left undone for me.
The front lawn is littered with white packing peanuts
& wet toilet paper, left clinging to the rocks & formerly bare arms of the palo verde.
This blizzard was made for me, is potentially the last time I complain
about missing the snow to all of my asshole friends.

Trash bag in hand, headphones on, walkman hiccuping, surling
as a dark gray spills 'cross the horizon.
                & of course now — rain.

& understandably
I am aware that I am, in fact, a cartoon of myself.
The comedy of this moment is not lost on me —
the laughable folly of thinking this prank
the vessel I am born into
is a gift — artfully laid out for me
unknowing of what this present
would leave untwined — the thought squirming
in the nest I've made, in plain hiding,
& foolishly shared.

I should've never shown any part of myself to anyone.
I receive the gesture, and am left alone to celebrate it.
If they knew me better they might understand that

I cannot even leave through the door without first romancing the window.
Without intent to make all these loose ends somehow fashionable, damn

I already spent all morning raking every inch of me —
leaving tight bags of hair to be taken away
no longer hitched to this body
struck from the brick wells until they dew red and get choked
by bits of paper.
Every pore pledges to the wind *never again, never again*
& drowns out the music.

I already look like an unfortunate mummy, the best I could budget for.
If I were to laugh I would not hear it, but the moment *is* profound —
clearing tissue just for it to fall off of me into the brush.

I feel like a cheap frog — like this skin dreams in wet tongues.
But I will now keep my wants to myself for the rest of my days.

I can't forget things —
my partner said to me once *I'd love the girl in you if you leveled this forest* &
I shaved my whole body until it bled for years
stared into the mirror as droplets slip down my arms
and fell with the sound of light pebbles to the carpet
&   let my trust stay fragile.

I remember the terrarium, too. How I made it a
home with good intention, scuttled after many a
baby frog with a cup to save them from the wild —
believing what I was doing was valiant, with the cold season ever closer.
Unaware of how the frog crawls into
the earth, slows, sleeps through the cold in solitude — sounds nice.

I shiver already, can't shake the closet —
the heavy clothes I put on thick as mud
to hide my shape, as I do the born body,
the earthen labor I struggle to survive in my name with confidence.

I cannot forget
my sister curious and kind — reached for the cage
and in loving embrace buried all of my stolen guests
in small rocks and bowls, rooms made for them.
But who was to blame? — more me than her.

Though I rise in spring, however haggard —
trust remains.

I cannot forget all the times
I have been buried in my own house.
& so, my friends, take the key from me gently — I am trembling.

I am letting you in because winter   is already with me
wherever it is   I happen to be.

RE: HOUNDS OF LOVE I

Dog — *Bark*
      Fox — *Yip*
Yup, all bare teeth
in born-fur.

It is a big
wonder whether
I am the fox
      or the hound it runs from.
It chases me until I am
      out of breath.

People say "unclench your jaw,"
      but I force my molars together 'til they split like brooms.
I do not
      know
            what
                  is good for me, understand?

I used to pull
      at my
            my chin
                'til I exposed
                    my sharp bottom teeth.

The torn bits betwixt
them could identify my hunger,
but *shh* — I know
it is obvious.

The bits of red
now where the body was,
shimmer —
stain my collar.

Beauty is all
      from wild clay
the same cold, wet earth
as feeling sought after
              or unwanted.

Loving yourself
is a shape at the end of a
        long
                hook,
an unknowable   murk
until the surface   breaks.

Listen — I talk to myself.

I say things like
Oh you sweet huntress,
     livin' the dream one day at a time
  (EPIPHANIES).
        You ugly dog-shape!
           Yip — jagged smile!
               Bark — shattered water!

All I can piece together sometimes
is the shadow of a will.
Its contour scares me
      always rises
           slowly,   blindingly
like bones
     in the yard —

         buried.

LET'S EXCHANGE THE EXPERIENCE

My Quingdom for a moment
in which Kate Bush is slowly lowered
from the ceiling above me.

My Quingdom for a miracle.

Instead, I just stand —
my arms stretched above me,
in spotlight, waiting.

Instead of this performance,
this everyday performance where
I settle for the opening shift,
I could stand
in *your* place, say nothing
            when you ask about my morning,
exchange currency   and then leave.

Maybe I could ask
"Who is this,"
point to the ceiling,
                and exit before the answer.

And then instead of rain maybe hot coffee,
or simply the privilege of
choosing either/and/or again
each morning
        instead
            of feeling this far away.
        Instead
            my loves — they never that once & I
            feel left here forever.

Okay.
We never until we do.
Instead we settle for the opening shift
even after the performance
 wherein we Do, and Do Sometimes
    until we Never — that's the life we didn't choose.

But
My Quingdom for a Late Night
without an Early Morning.

My Quingdom for you too,
Instead of Nevering that once,
to stand in front of me —
   even in silence.

Instead   morning   always.
Instead
currency comes and goes like rain
& we sometimes
                    in spotlight inherently or for a wage.

Instead, my arms out stretch
   & bodies recede into the ceiling above me —
        the Nevering, common as a cup of coffee
           relentless, relentless
   & the Always I wake to again,
and again is stage-view
               to a bare & echoing room.

I could've stayed home just this once,
but instead you say
          not even to me but near enough for me to hear
that you
could never see loving a body like mine
(unknowingly, sure)
& I am paid to just stand there —
     listening like a row of empty chairs.

What could I do but just
turn the music up,
and stare into the ceiling,   waiting for you to leave?

What all I have done just
to hear all that and keep still-ing.
What all I have done in performance,
but remain every part of me all the same
        on and off stage
            and here, with you.

Kate Bush plays and you dare to ask
    "Who   is   this?"
I would never tell.
    I   will   *never*   tell   you
                                        forever.

When so many of us are gone,
    & the miracle is the stilling, here —

You do not get my Quingdom
    when you promise not   to love me.

ANISE (COCHITOS)

Make our miracles of earth / smirk with the morning sweet
the thick of molasses —
A burn that lingers long enough to confess
it was worth to reach
in secondhand stores.
Heavy carts,
in clear mugs fulfilled with coffee,
   hot,
   50 cents less
              down there —
Wherever we can find it,
really.

Whatever bin you can reach into
and pull out your hands
              pregnant with stars.

SMALL THINGS AND ALL AFTER THEM (DANIEL)

Don't eat all the bees, Daniel.
Science says there are only so many left — *like maybe at least 12.*
I have a tentative grasp of science
& I'm likely to believe that which is fact only when not proven wrong.
Ya know kid? *Science.*

> Like, prove to me that pie is
> not just fruit soup
> in a bread bowl.

That's not, *not* a fact.
And so — I am forever justified to eat
my fill of pie in the throws of a fever
and seasonally   in late fall and winter.

That's a fact. A good one.
It is fall now and I am pie-less.
(A sad fact)
It is winter just past my shirts — a fact, for
        what is beautiful to me does not flower here.

So. My science is not my love's, I believe. (Pending)
Leaves begin to fall here and   (to my understanding) never touch salt.

A leaf accepts change. (Pending)
Waking with the sun and swinging a hammer to make change produces salts.
Falling and waking to the same salts
has me, a leaf, stuck between fall and winter, and
the waiting before a fall is *endless.* (Pending)

I know you can touch two oceans, both of salts, in half a day
with intent. It is proven. (Fact)

Feeling suspended between seasons is an endless salt and that too can be a comfort —
The waiting before the Fall.

Salts are delicious — (Proven) and lead in some way to pie, I am told.
I am terrible at baking (Definitely) but I trust a love's taste
for my salts and accept their science for fact.
When I can.

Bees communicate with a series of awkward dances. (Fact) Also (Same).
Fire too dances, (true) but not for bees —
still mimics the bold stretch of wing and body
flirting with the wind, suspended
comfortably, stuck between seasons.
Before the fall.
I know there is loss I've yet to meet. (Pending)
I know fire dances across a pie not yet done and makes it complete by some science.

Queer Joy is a science I have no grasp of just yet.
I believe it is a salt before a flame,
a last bee humming a fire song
making bloom with each awkward dance —
And yet elusive to the calendar,
suspended between seasons.

(Fact) Of course each small thing
amounts to something.
A leaf falls and suddenly a warm harvest.
A love sees me as I am
and dances in two oceans
                              in just twelve hours.
(Praise)
How salts leave the body and make change —
go from desert to where leaves wait for them just to fall. (Proven)

One can reach for a pie still
dancing with the fire
and assume it burns. As the years do. As winter does.
As does searching your body for a season it was not born into. (Proven)
Our hands, I think cannot know sweet
as the tongue does, (Fact)
but can touch lips
learn dances — pull out the plate to share with a love.
Bless each air-kissed foot for the pie before us.
The all-sweet this Queer has Wrought.

It is profound to believe in another's science.
That maybe you cannot not live
forever in another's mouth.

Don't prove me wrong.

There are already very few bees left.
                                   So few tiny moments before we fall again.
But oh how all that
is not yet gone
                    works to give us everything.   (Proven)
I have —
          everything.

                              (Fact)
I do.

So cool it, Daniel.

Re: Hounds of Love II

You know, I
   was always running — even as
                     a pup in the Georgian sun —
each fist of red earth was chucked
at passing cars.   *What chase!*
We hid behind small mountains
like weedlings
     and yelped in hushed dandelion voices, goodness:

Let me show you what I carved
into this rock   with   a rock.
  It's a deer at the water's edge, yeah?
                     Do you see it?
  Yup, just as I found it — 100 feet tall.
Made small here for you, forever.
Yup, don't come around much — you know.   Jump easy, but I'm real   real quiet.
Shh! Leave your shoes, before you scare them off.   Throw them into the lake!
Let everything we leave behind be fashion for tadpoles!
          We cannot let anyone find this or follow.   If anyone
finds this they will come for us,   the wild will be done for.   But we
can take shelter   behind trees   in basements   under rolling shapes —
Trust me!   My friend, I trust you.
Listen!
       Run!
           RUN!
      That cloud
             looks   just   like   a kiss!
I've been told that a kiss
        is dangerous.

PINCH (MARIA LUISA)

Morning is the ringing —
the Tolleson bell & intuitive crows of the neighbors' roosters
who wake one. just. after. the. other. after. the. other.
pulling at the dawn like flour.

Tortillas turn charcoal over
the open stove — left & not forgotten.

She speaks so often of her brothers
who would beat the sun just to grab
the top few fresh tortillas from the stack
one. after. the. other. after. the. other.
& their names rise & fall like nylon strings,
hang on the wall like smoke — turn
the photos salt & lime, salt & lime.

For her mother, who had many sons,
there was never enough time.
Morning was to pinch the flour
again, and again
like a ringing —   I think it wakes me.

I may never get these back,
I am told (these moments).
The rosy hours I give to the dough,
to stretch and stretch the flour thin
to place each one. atop. the. other.
It's the tower I sing from
the line I cast
to keep you with me, today.
Although I fear
all that will stay here,   is the smell of ash.

Rabbit

"You must know me, Father it's your son
And I know that you are proud
Of everything I've done
But it's the wonders I perform,
Pulling rabbits out of hats
When sometimes I'd prefer
Simply to wear them"
—Paddy McAloon

I've been spending a lot of time
considering the astrological sign of my pet rabbit,
who, on the morning of our leaving (Summer 2016),
I woke to find lying soft and unmoving.
Which was, to me, a really Pisces way
of announcing that they would not be
making the journey, though it did
grant us a moment to rest still
between roofs to run under —
Our worth just of our pelts in trade,
my life in bags on the curb.   His — a mound in the sunflowers.

Father what will I be to you
   when the hard wheels inside me
   cease to answer to *Son,* or Turn?
What small thing will I be?   I'm worried *here* and then *gone* as fast.

I can't help but remember you tending to the roof.
Your ladder, by accident, broke through a hidden nest
of bunnies in the yard — soft kin left dressing the grass
suddenly then, even softer.   It wasn't your fault.

Will you ever forgive me for that?
you ask.

                    & I sit there, carelessly silent.

When I was younger we would talk for hours
      pretending to fish off the porch in Tucson.
            Reeling in twin fish, red snapper —
                  Pulling the ocean from the sand with laughter
'til the sun sprung to rest in its hutch.
Pulling life from dust is and was miraculous, but what of language?

Say only to me now the magic of my love's name.
You don't need to say *sorry* just
honor that I come to you as prey
    begging for better-than-careless grandeur.
                                    We can make it a simple incantation —

That would be a wonder   I would live so loud for.

Please —   Of course, I remember and can forgive you —
can let soft things lay in peace,
but honor me now.   Simple.

Do you not feel a daughter's fur   in my hands?
Do you not know
                        how long
                                I can stay quiet?

ARE YOU MY YOUNGEST BROTHER, OR MY YOUNGEST SON?

she asks my father,
laughs hot-air-balloon when he takes off the mask

if these are the clouds you are dwelling in
I love for me, these eyebrows
I love for you, my sisters & brother
who are so much the best of everyone here —
kindest heart and kindest heart
     sharer, teacher

the sun, the sun, the sun
the answer is — our youngest suns amongst us
to think —   we just have them
to think —   we get to learn them every day
                    how kind of them to fall from the sky
                    & share a couch, instead

I Don't Dance — I Have Sex With Strangers

I am trying, in my quiet way, to be known,
but I struggle to find the words
when she asks "Do kids still dance? Do... you, dance?"
The omission, to me, feels more honest.

Truthfully
even when the Hammer of Life stands still
I throw myself, iron-hot against it & anyone
begging *change me, change   me,   make me malleable,*
    but I cannot tell her that.
    I do not want to be this   throat-dammed   kettle-eyed
            collar-beige —

a falsehood cairn /
in constant danger of falling apart completely
like a tall bowl of oranges.
Gosh   that is likely much for anyone, let alone my own legs —
they go tinder-buckle in the heat of the night.   So no — I do not often
dance,
but I say *yeah   yeah, sometimes.* Love I find is better carried by open arms
        unburdened by the juggle of *total* transparency.
   Well actually I don't believe that, but
   I mean — how much do you *really* want to know, Abuela?
     Each tiny, not-a-lie is a clasp
to keep me, a *single me* so let us not shine the light too brightly hither.
Once I caught
   the waning moon splitting my shadow in three
   & found the dark selves only —
Do you follow? I *already* drag my feet but you know this!
I have my tells — my sweat goes sweet,
   my vowels limp, calls & prayers unanswered. I do want better for us
    I do,   *I do,*
I want whatever faith fills Tia Helen's house with porcelain roosters
or keeps the earth mill-tilling my feet to powder.
But when this morning comes
     and the sun does its setting
     I can't help but notice she already carries too much
        to possibly hold on to.

I watch her go through her purse in circles
      go through the kitchen all through the night
           go out into the yard and back, lock the doors, unlock the doors
rummage through all my packed bags
thinking, maybe, I only *just* got here   instead of me, leaving.

She makes all my belongings constellation across the house
hangs my ready-shirts, scatters my tiny treasures.

To calm her mind I say I am coming back.
          I love it here.   *I am coming back soon.*
I leave in the morning,
          but I am coming back   *soon.*
And when she washes my gifted knife dull & white
          I say   *these small things mean as small to me*
it's fine   *it doesn't matter*
and then   —   the worry gone   like the simmer   off the flame
the untruth opened
          like the copper round my wrist —
          one of the few links
            that tethers me to this withholding earth.
These small things mean as small to me.

She asks   *wait — where are you going, again?*
And I say
          dancing.

CALLOUSED PALMS, CALLOUSED PSALMS

For Manuel Anthony

The sound a hammer plays,
swinging a pipe into the cold desert ground,
is so sweet, so hollow (so sweet).

La Maria doesn't stand too proud this
warm, warm winter
but wears the earth so pretty,
shawled in a flat green light,
expression lost for a time —
stolen and returned (once more) white.

"That'll do" my grandfather says
managing our placement
of reindeer & green cord around her.

I am certain, we understand each other —
where quit lives & doesn't live in the heart,
how to grab the ghost by the tail
(when you mean the collar)
what to do with the losses
that time makes music *with*
    & *not with* you sometimes — that's all there is.
For him — a wound, a wound, a wound
  For me — a wound (a wound), a wound
     the ways we are played, are still playing
      The dark we lay in is not an absence of song.

It is good enough,
to wear the shirt you kept living in
and be lucky *at* the world.

Better to be ugly *at* than *to it*
Better to be quiet than say something you regret.

I know he knows my smirk for it is his smirk
I know he knows our pain for it is his pain
though I see the ways he labors to keep it.

The Work,
This Work — however humble,
  is safer than gambling,
     safer than drinking.
    Plugging hole by hole (in our own way) daily
lest the rain fully flood the house and
tin-pan timpani through the night (and night).

I work (this learned work) in prayer —
  take two hands worth of lawn
   & run it through my face and hair.

Every time I travel back home
I can only hope he looks at me
   & hears any music like his own.

Sees my sweat
and the good Lord in it.

Re: Hounds of Love III

Boots press into soft autumn snow
& autograph our leaving through
November and November, new.

Hard year.
    No flowers to speak of,
save the shadows of tiny paws.
Save the beavertail in the marsh
the mugwort by the train tracks, clicking in the breeze.

Time sprouts
    a coward's bar tab, curls in its length —
Barks *Maddog!* Barks *20/20!* Blooms in the tub blood red.
Jokes *How Gay* —
    I can't quite see straight! Barks *Bark!*

Feeling anything is ever   all budding
                    is so false   and bold.
In these infant hours
      these old days *Bark* solemn wonders.

Past nights stretch a quiet between angry tums.
We know 2am is for the cold & hungry
has brought me
      a neck in my teeth,
      and a neck in my teeth, and a neck in my teeth
& mine in another
         & torn fur from absent shirts. *Yip!*

Past days shed my body thin
So *Yip*, I bark —
    Look back when you can.
I bark *Bark!*
      at all these shadows I do not understand

         No matter what passes
through or with us —   see me
& you   in what we leave behind.

I dare you to see me in the hunted and hunter,   although I run from this.

Look back —

I dare you to tell the claws apart
                                   by the tracks.

6/30/22

I am trying to my put my finger
   on the map of it all
            but the math
            makes no sense to me —
                        A knuckle for every mile of river?
                        So what? I nick my thumb cutting fruit
                        & am both less river & more fruit? Is that right?
I wet the cotton brick with minutes
& have already lost a lifetime to thought, *oh God!*
I don't have time for this!
I may very well be the last of my blood so *glory!*
                  Glory, somehow I
                  still make more of me!

When I begin to swell I put the work in
take account of the earth's turning
by the mass in my leg.
            It grows and grows and by the end of the year,
            I am months from hip to knee.

After it is taken from me, I close one eye
& imagine myself down there
                    traveling the cut
                    braving the bruising rapids rather
                    than remaining here in fear.

I'd like to see the throughlines in my own body as clear.

When the back screams
      NORTH   SOUTH!
NO, SOUTH!   NORTH —   NORTH SOUTH!
      NORTH! NORTH!

I break sweat, panicked for rest

spun and turned rubik by the hands of time
forever awake to all my
bad habits.
            I bite my nails.
            I cut my bridges in the pursuit of growth — *funny!*

If all the times I have begged, just this year, for help
could roll back into my person
like tape would that not be my ascension?

Wouldn't you be all the *more* proud of me?
                I'm not trying to be aloof, promise
                I'm just unfathomably tall
                in the neck!   I can't hear you up here!
Is it not   *your job to help me?*
                        I can't *hear* you!

            For whatever help I do get
                I am so lucky.
I am reminded, by lovers and doctors, that I am   *so lucky*
                  to let others' hands simply travel me.
52 from Fall River
                kindly sends photo after unsolicited photo of himself &
                It is such a relief to know   *exactly*   where *he*
                begins   and   ends!
Thank you, 52!
                It can be known!
At least,
I've found the capital of my
industrious sprawl,   *but to what end?*
Who do I owe my thanks to for the   vantage of solitude?

I'm already holding the mayor of my multiple 'tudes hostage
& giving out keys to the city —   *Just write me!*   *Anytime!*
I am so tired holding open for passage!
I spend all of my time with the captive self &
I can   and do   say almost   *anything!*

Just ask my hurting friends.
                    I see we are all so, so lonely of course —
                    social only like boats in the dark.
Touch seems such a sinking thing, but
                    I need to share this wave with you tonight.

I wish I could see how close we are far apart
                more than sometimes.
I wish, for all of us, to better understand —
                that to be lost at one another is
                        hilariously impossible.

I wish I did not lose so much time to the unknown
                    to reaching out to the wrong people.

If I could get it all back
                    I would be miles in the cloud
                    with all of that endless sight.
                    (& what little I have now)
                                I would happily give it to all of you
                                        inch by inch,
                                            hand by hand
                                                river   by river.

I Know, in Some Ways, I Must Be Answering for All the Times I Begged for More Time in My Kitchen

When the sun peels from my living bones to reveal
a forever dark I've heard of — dress me in lemon.

I am not let back to my home for a week
& my houseplants lean like ovened herbs in butter.
These times are loud-smell and out of breath, leaning on my weak.

Where on the tongue does the will live?

I am trying to unstuck
sour candy from the gap in my teeth,
but all these moving parts grow wider.

Got the molar out finally before it curled my skull into a hurt diamond.
Was in and out of the office in just an hour.
Time makes funny deposits like salt rings true in the maw.
What has flavor or weathering wrought
other than a hole in my mouth and born-debt?

I am worth 63 whole American dollars, but
all I wanted was to be rich in hours.

Now I am hoarding groceries,
pawing at lively shapes lest they bruise and ripple
in their own undoing — I can't blame them,
but I bloat with these gifts.

I do my best to get full
three times daily.
Bless these segmented days. Cubed hours. Stolen watch-stock.

Is this what we meant when we asked for things to slow down for just a minute?
I've got questions at the business end of a 3-hour phone queue.

Besides many things,
what does a knife do that
a reflection does not do to my sense of well being?

How can I brush my eye back into a tasteful shape or
pour the warm of me into the palm of my bed
without crying?

How does one plate a ghost for vespers?
What's a hymn but a course for reckoning?
What oil is safe to wet my rosary
and if the people
    are hungry and looking in — what do I charge them?

Lord,
sweet Lord,
    if this is life with all my prayers
                        answered
                            then eat me.

Pull the Rail

What
        would you expect of me —
                other than to walk into
                the mouth of a train

Where, in sorrow
        you went to play the Crispin coin
                rested 'neath
                your wary tongue
thankfully,
        only
            for but a moment

What else
        was I to do
                when I heard its iron body, calling
                from my window —
a neighbor to the waking dark

I hoped
        it was
                a toothache
                for what else
        makes a grown thing
        cry into the night

Or rather
        what of those do I
                have any idea
                of how to remedy

Please
        let it be just that

What
        act of comfort
                could snuff the fire
                too gone from the shell

Please
        allow me to beam at my
                gloves, bare
                grin at the heavy pliers —
        thirsty for iron molars

It is penny-wish
        to fill my bowl with whistles
                of our shared time
                (it gallops in me)

My friend
        what you gift to me
                gives these walls a pulse —
                sparing me from strangers' mouths

It would be such a silly thing to attempt —
                        taking to the rails

Me without my license
                and all

RE: THE BIG SKY

I don't know what to tell you.

Morning breaks over
me and I cannot
reach for the hot glass without
my hands shaking. You offer yours,
but how do I grasp back
without alarming you to my inherent rigidity?

Hello. I'm trying to do my best
work with the shapes inside me. Okay?

I can't always be responsible for my sharpness
& I need to know if I've hurt you.

I'm trying, trying to make myself
a better person through the soft
dad-hands of my barber, and I can't
let him see me cry yet. Oh.
He scrapes the bristle from my
throat and I am so thankful
for my mug so smooth, ravaged,
winter-cold with menthol upon my quick leaving.

There's an inherent violence to all of this
I think, gazing out over a fleeting
New Hampshire. Window-side, I am
seduced by the gut-heavy blue.

Kiss me on my big spiny mouth, Nashua!

Stop me if this turns you on, but
    what is God's whole, omnipotent, deal?
Does the plan exist to till my
spirit or are my roots just coming up?
I hear the whining, but won't call back, I am sure.
I'll get to it in time
and in time — even more so.

I didn't pay $33 to be alone on this bus
but I don't get to choose anyone, ever.

Not even the light I return to.
Not even when to wake, really.
I'm trying, trying
so hard, all the time
to not let my body harbor debt
without consent. But when I wake
coins spill off of me —
        peel off my back and dance away through the kitchen.

I crush an egg into the pan
(a smaller sun over a small sun)
and I get to keep living most
uncertain of the cracks in things.
Promises still get made
        and time makes them into
                angry ransom letters.

This hurts me,
but I vow to never eat cheese again
in daylight.

I eat a whole pizza in the dark

and finally weep one morning
at a single tree erupting
with birds who twist and burst
into the soft, bashful sky.

What a gift!
What a relief it would be to
be simply broken &
yet I still remain
so wildly
and dangerously whole!

GIFTED — ORANGES

I've known
a sunny day after
too long a time of wanting.
But now, from the yard,
I think just
as much of a gentle gray
linen, pulled 'cross
the morning pink, in tenderness.

It is all of simple things —
the loud comfort
of shedding.

A soft wind makes
a partner of the pecan tree
& I wake to your
memory, crashing through
my roof as thick branches.

No one hears the pruning
until, in time, spring gifts the
body with colorful swellings.
We stand in awe of its loudness.

You've made a window of me
with fist/home-ish song
& now I see the orange.
I taste the oranges —
bite through the bitter
pores, skin & all.
Leave nothing for the
heavy hands of rain
to take (with ease).

The soft breeze of your
name has already
plundered me,
I swear, & has left
not a thing
that will not
grow loudly.

Aerosmith (Dream On)

I won't believe I've got so much to do with Steven Tyler
Not if I have a mouth in this well/
Anything to do with this nightmare bar.
I'm drowning I think (*so often* I think)
when somebody says to me *nice fella like you here*
and we exchange a pulse or some numbers
when all I have to spare is a hollow chuckle.

If God put a jukebox in this brick dumpster,
I'd have *such* A Big Nothing to say —
I'd have so much work to do with all the cold tile in Manchester.
Bet I could build a bridge from your quiet hands to my profile in fireworks.

Bet one whole dollar no one here sees me above
the roaring ashtray cloud of my passing body & it makes sense to me —
why people press against each other so aggressively
'gainst stage edge
            see themselves
                in glitter drum head.
For a moment believe they are
the *boom*   *boom*   *boom!*   folks run toward
                               and not away from.
Bet Mr. Tyler sees just above a thousand brows and feels me from far 'cross town.
How that must feel — to know nothing of what it is when you kiss
me, four quarters, drink in hand.

All the times I've held you with me I've felt you hear my sweat speak,
wailing from the spring it rang from
Joyous, Joyous
         like
           I'll   never have   to hear
                           Dream On   again.

And good.
Fuck that song.

RE: MOTHER STANDS FOR COMFORT

I would hope that if	You saw me for my soft wants	You'd be proud
Nothing else, you'll understand	I know you did once	
One day that no one	Asked for that photo of us	
Wants me to be different	Carried it with me —	Left the house
More than me — that's just a fact	Made each new home	Whole

I am careless, sure	Raised with a warm grace	
But it's in my caring that	You made a nothing	Into a star
I seem to hurt y'all	Maybe a blessing	Glow & Bloom
The most I can do is to be	What you must have wanted	
Gentle, honest	More than just a whisper	

Sometimes I think to	Ask for your patience	Simple
Call you — to no avail	I'm not well today	Simple as that
We connect only when we	Wake to our sprouts rain-drowned.	
Sound hollow and fruitless	I can't tell you that	(Simple)
Uncertain of the point	I can't open my mouth	

You have to know I	Want so much more from me too	Daily
Want more than this, but I can't	Find the peach, the joy (I try)	I try
Bring this to seed to harvest	Amongst the pits, I am trying	To See
My hands are so	Careless, as I am, I am trying	
Cold and dirty I tried, I am	So tired, but I am trying	To See the Sun

CAMPFIRE

Across from you
I wonder how long to go without
bringing attention to the small
thumb of charcoal on your lips.

You say to me
  All of this,
    All of this not possible without us.
Tomatoes rupture and
leave orange constellations —
starfish to the cool bamboo placemats.

3 or maybe 4 sun-rusted
leaves amongst the many
say
  All of this,
    All of this
& mean that rain is coming.

I would go through
the worst of all of it again
to be what I am for you, now.
I'm sure you know.

We ran from fire, into
the White Mountains for
  All of this,
    All of this
again and entwine —
Two embers in a cast iron knapsack.

After my mouth on you,
I think of not washing my face
again, for a long time.
Proudly wearing
  All of this,
    All of this
maybe into the world, the gas station, the train.
And so linger my eyes
on your lips, again
and think to leave the charcoal
at least for now.

Before August was
a long, long time.
Wet logs need just as much to catch and murmur —
I hadn't known
I could run away and also towards something.
Each heavy foot just swung past the other.
Each booted pendulum whispered
   All of this,
      All of this not possible without us
against the wind.

And kicked up no ashes.

RE: CLOUDBUSTING

*"The idea of a sunflower is the only thing about
a sunflower that glows in the dark."*
— Eric Dovigi

I sit to put on my boots —
daydreaming on the same corner you used to
rest till we slept, & I swear
the slope of my bed — a whole coast away
indents to mirror your weight.
The whole of your stories, unfinished,
soft fairytales.

The nature of the vast between us
    is folkloric — exists in joy, but the absence
    is Brass-Clad. Is Stone-Boney. Crushes me like
    I am the last whisper of marigold under
        the iron-cool shadow
                of a thunderstorm.

When my hair was long & curly, night & fire
    you used to tell me I was beautiful
    like a musketeer.
& still when I shaved it all off.
& still.
Not knowing this is all I wanted to be to anyone,
    lamenting the long dresses and satin I threw away to live here with you
    to keep dry of your salt rain, or so I thought.

1942. Willhelm Reich builds a machine for
    producing rainclouds before he is abducted in front of his son.
Left a cloudbuster without a master
& the magic of the thing leaves with the absence of its dreamer.

2016. 2017. 2018. They say tired. They say blood sugar.
They say dementia. They say family. They say Alzheimer's,

& now my memory of your stories is desperate
    & the wonders of my heart seem a quiet story to an empty bed.

I think so often of your wide range of yarns to spin
    & worry to what end time unwinds you.

I look still in shock
     at the empty gaps in my closet
staring back at me like the blue between clouds,
woven and torn apart in jagged monument —
& think it must be miles more than we can even see,
     between these known places to rest.
To what end do I tell you of this Queer
     when I fear more of my heart will leave with you, *Pues Mida.*
All trans bodies tear through the white satin / ocean whisper
          hand in hand
                    on leaving.
               Cloudbusters with no hand at the wheel
               & can't you see my shape among them? *Mida!*

Pues, I think to call
          and tell you everything again.
Gift to you my new name,
and be beautiful still
the glow of a story
after the life of its teller.
But I sit on the edge of the bed
and hang my mouth open
     quiet as the waiting Earth before the water drops.

ANAL

The conversation of *who* is entering *who* —
who turns the knob when the door is knocked —
has no place here
between two Queer bodies,
two writhing arches turning top sheet
dull in color, but

a raucous shoreline to our monumental union in hot salts.

No need to hold the applause, but once we'd reached proudly
into each other and in victorious recline their
back popped in a roar of granite-split —
my hand in the small of their shoulder blades
and eyes toward the fan at the far door.

Before this hot room, a hotter desert and no A/C in
the car, unhindered. No means to outrun the hulking flame, the sun, the close star,
the biggest thing we can see both sides of, maybe.

They say everywhere's the same, but in Boston the summer
is a scalding tongue in my ear.
A violent mutter.
I walk the street and check my shoulder into a stranger who calls me a slur
on my commute, names my kindling body for what it is in passing.
And we both go home wet anyway.

I am done with humidity. The Arizona sun was at least an honest one.
What it took from me it did with sharp hands, tore at my skin, relentless
as others took and left no candle for the shrine.

There is no honor, but a comfort in feeling unwelcome
everywhere, when no one calls you anything.

But here you call my name
                              like I gave it to myself.

Like we two are manifest of all open windows,
all reckless tumbling rocks into
cool, clear water —
              ankle deep, navel deep,
stone upon stone into
                    geode-revealing clatter.

The sound of every disc
       as it pops is an unlocked door,
       and then another   &   another
& suddenly —
     all of our house is open to moonlight tenants
& each breath
       frees a cool breeze —
           the first sip of relief from a stone door.
A temple of fresh air
       welcomed into, and not simply entered.
No handle,
      no hinges,
          just home.

(click) !

RE: THE 9TH WAVE (B)

"We are of the Going Water
and the Gone
We are of Water
in The Holy Land of Water"

RE: AND DREAM OF SHEEP

I sleep & wake in fits of anchor, still

& could know comfort by the bell of iron on sand

& wade in cold hands — crossed over knees, or cradled in linen

& what of comfort — what *wish this woulds* tower over me?

& what of the shadow of the thing — and not it, itself?

& what is hope but a bow against this field of ice? forgive my break

& my loved ones' names are stars to my aidless sight
                    are sour to my stomach lurched over sweet
                    are the leverage to the bottle cap & the fizz — *greedy much?*

& who could hold my wander without drowning too, anyway
                    that's enough out of you,   *truly — enough*

& whose mouth could embrace my name and buoy, still
                    I can hear you saying all of us, all of us,   *any of all of us*

& praise this ageusia for partnering my soul-thirst
                    say that again   *no really — say it*

& bless the far shore for being just that   *sure, far enough is far*

& know the wolf in the mirror more than I do sleep

However close I need it to be   I am hungry. hungry to dream

3/1/21

I've come to notice that in my dreams
                        all your hairs are   *smaller.*

Why you don't use my waking hours to grow them I don't understand.
   These things take time, sure.
                            And rest (sure)!

Come on,
      I will cook you the most brilliant egg —
soft & running gold.

What are you doing for joy lately?

                     I am discovering.

I've learned that I love myself most honestly
when I remember napkins before
I need napkins,
that I feel most loved — wordlessly gifted tinned fish or lime.

I am sleeping and then my eyes stay open when I wake —
      I am afraid of what they are telling people beyond my intent.

My own curls are growing back and hopefully soon
will interlace with yours like fingers.

I am trying to stop harvesting all my herbs before I plant them —
These things take time.

I am saying *I am doin' my best at doin' my best.*
I am saying   *I am doin' my best at doin' my best.*
I am saying   *I am doin' my best at doin' my best.*

Every day

I am struggling to touch the earth
      without dreaming of a hand to hold.

THIS FAR OUT, I CAN NEVER TELL WHETHER THE SUN RISES OR SETS — THE ANSWER (I KNOW) IS BOTH, BUT I FORGET (SUNSET I)

All these miracle worlds   in the broth —
All we can   know   between the finger and thumb
                                        penny
                                        pearl
                                        patterned tile.
Phoroptic view —
                the jewel beneath the brow.
All we can   know   is drum on the wind   (the wind that easy carries)
                        cherries copper on the tongue
                                        elbow-deep in poppy seeds.
Every window should open
                every song can be a window, open
                                to fall through
                                to crow from.
Hello! Hello Earth
                        Are you seeing   me?
                            What stories   are   you?
                                Can   you share?
                                Please   can you share them
                                                with me?

SUNSET II

I burst out of my shirt with
grape liquor — slept in the yard and woke speckled,
each ruby a kiss where blood was taken, each day a new day where
blood was taken — no answers. No answers for months upon months, it
swelled on my spine, hot crimson — I cried through the night so I tore it out.
I tried but it returned in my leg, stirred like a hard cloud — drowned out the light.

Re: Under Ice

Holy night, do not touch me.
So many swans
in frightening numbers stay close atop the mirror, haunting.

Sparklers — little bugs of comfort
in different flightful moments
          show us a small a-gasp in each of us
          & I think that's why they make them.
          someone hands one to me and so I hand it to someone else
          saying I thought you would like one
freed my second hand for a second tall can.

New year, new year, new year
blew the fuse of comfort (this one).
Ran the oven till it coughed up birds for my friends.
They left full & rang it in.
When they left I
dug out the driveway &
my love from towers of fabric &
Legos in the carpet   oil paints in the ceiling   ash in the fan, ash in the
bathtub.
I promised I'd leave as soon as the apartment
glowed as if I was never

                                        there.

I cried *don't you want this to be different*
          aren't you sick of this
                    you must be sick of this — you have to be!
But I left all the plants
to keep their reach towards the windows.
     I looked back at the foggy glass & saw it written

                                        never again.

I kept saying
     never again
          never again
          until I forgot and it was past time to go anyway   & so I did.

I Put This Moment, Here

I hear nothing but
the sound of hoofs
           your chest reeling with salinous bravery.
The desert held us for a brief moment
                open window
the memory rises in me
marigold and beaming   with dark eyes closed
              morning bleak even.
You dance through my hallways
           post-saddle and unknowing
           what stood firmly locked before
           my hostel spirit knew the company
           of your gentle steps.
Hush now, you'll hear the bars
           of broken morning light play your sharp cheeks.
           Hush now, the foal laps at the water —
           a melody to your falling tears
Hush now — we can not stay here
           for the rest of time, I'm sorry.
Quietly fill your pockets with earthen treasures,
           bundled creosote on the dashboard.
           Hush now — I feel you shuffling through the night
           and hear all of spring's gay applause.
We're not leaving.
           We are not leaving, quite yet.
           I am home in your welcome name
                so forever
                so forever the west unfurls inside of me
                so forever amidst all the everything you give to me.
           We will have the memory of wild horses at dawn
                (which I gave to you & would again).

Sunset III

Bless Pete's Fish and Chips
in the Phoenix Valley — their foil pans of
onion rings, fries piled high — for 10 cents back then.
For my grandparents, a not so small joy   even still   for me,
my last dollars for a burger after driving to Tolleson to teach the
day after the election. No child, no child should look in such a huskish way.
The teller winks at me, he asks if there's anything else I need. I say so much so
so so much more, for all of us, but how can we make this moment last forever?

AM I THE CAT THAT TAKES THE BIRD?

I can see what stands between us,
of course I can —   the way I am loving
you is to, every hour, build a bridge.
I am loving you for why you are, today.
I am writing you to say that I love you
in this way, but I do not ask you to make the
trek more than to acknowledge the door, open.

The thoughtful hand is a gift you gave me
as is the flourish of the tether — how I look at a vase,
or bring together flowers is my inherited way   I do my best
to tell you about what I am building with your tools —
          the home I am dreaming of & the path to it.
But I do not cross to meet you
more than the annual toe by toe closer —
So I am not doing my best.

RE: WAKING THE WITCH

I am living in the flame of a tiny candle
                when I think of you the wick is lit
I tell you *I am thinking of you*, but you know
                            say I know, I felt it   *(I know you do)*

Out in the silt I search for
                the net of the world
                my hands shuffle to find the kite strings taut
                        to our lights divine
                        they charcoal flutter like a clarinet

My friends, I know you
                by the muddy leg
                    your darling snake
                        the offered (unasked for) hand
                            the bundled herb
                              & the arms aglow with nettle kisses
I know you because you ask things like
                        have you seen any good birds lately?
you know me because
                of course, I have   and know you will share in turn

Without a word I know you   let us quiet for a while

When I look out across the pond, y'all bobble
                        like apples in the night
                        fallen moons in the pewter wash

My friends — I beg you stay well & river-clean
                mind your toes for snapping turtles   *I am not joking*
I hold my breath
                midnight every dive beyond my line of sight
                      and *yes* I listen,
                      I heard you last time.

Friend,
I remember the way you sang from the car door   (at passing traffic)
                  It's a spell
                      do not hurt me or my friends
                thats a   *spell*

(I know there is no way it wasn't)
(I know it to be true)
(I feel this)

I feel you with me always
                    I wake thinking on you   & visit your dreams if you'll have me
I love you
                 every day   *I love you*

With all of   this   I am reaching out
               wading hip–deep into
               the water
               & pulling at
                   every ripple (as I wake to them)   like reigns

It's Just Loud Enough to Quiet My Mind

in solitude I spin the glass — it sings
the way we all wet our fingers moves me
tune me, turn the bolt — I am hot enough
wake up in the forge, fall asleep steaming
if there's a time to strike, I'm clocking in
and clocking in, and I'm clocking in, and
I'm clocking in, I am clocking in, and
when all the ice melts I'll walk everywhere
singing now from my winter throat, just wait
wait with me for my fears to ice-shatter
when you belt with me or sit in silence
the warmth glows a sound that nearly scares me
I beg the light *swallow* me my ears bleed
every day I am thinking of you, love

I'll take a picture next time
what're you up to my friend?
this hole in my pocket, burns
blow all of my bank account
hey now — I've been clocking in
hey now — I put the work in
you know — been meaning to call
we could go anywhere soon
soon is more than a word, yeah?
please I'm counting on you, friend
simply just to sit with you
is an opera to me
I sit alone, in quiet
can you hear me thinking, love?

SUNLIGHT IV

My hair goes in circles
coins of smooth with freckle — a sudden toll.
Today I am bringing me a kettle's worth of flowers. I am
shaving my head beautiful. I am prone to forgetting. I am prone
to losing this charmful life, though my altar is heavy with talismans,
each one a memory that I turn my thumbs over, place 'neath my pillows.
I drop one into the creek — it is lost at once amongst the rocks and minnows.
Each morning I visit the water like a grave I can't find — so I carry it with me.

TAMAL

each bead turned   is turned in prayer
each prayer turned a keychain   the lord with us on our thumb
we are all sons in the wrists   in the fields   gold & blue
maroon & pearl   in the creek stones clash & spark though I have no use for
them
I am throwing chile on the grill   I am waking tomatillo from its husk
I am tucking corn into bed   blisters soft my touch   salt over the
shoulder
              salt into the temples
              dream clean   dream clean   you have done so much
may we meet in the vast middle river
              please share with me everything when you wake
not to be so bold
I myself am just much too raptured   to sleep

SUNSET V

My brothers told me the
story of the bull's horn, but I don't recall
the story or where its long   first note landed — just that
the song would bring the stars to rest like cattle, like cattle slowly
coming home, but always leaving. You look like them you know? Their eyes
like your eyes — lost and amber,   lost and amber   warm & setting into me like a star

Re: Watching You Without Me

I wish you could say to me what you would when the arm of my missful river reaches
you (with tiny palms open).

In this dream you say *I am seeing you* as you might to a shell, plucked thoughtfully
from the glimmer.

Skipping stones curl to cup my rough and changing jaw (small fingers). I fear most
that you only sense a change in me.

You know me deeper than anyone. / Do you? / Do you like my haircut or does it
scare you as much as I am scared of it? / You can tell me that you don't know
my face today. / I don't know. / I do not. / You can tell me.

You can tell
        I don't know what to do   watching you   without me,
                                                            quiet sister.
        I don't.

Thumbtacks keep your dreams from curling off my purple walls. Faces with open
arms, bright wax circles on circles — speak *lift your chin up* to me.

When they become too precious — I do not see them. They sleep in a box until they
rise like clouds fresh from under pillows.

Can you know the lengths to which I keep your little lights alive
                                      or is that just a pearl for pockets?

I have this photo of Maria in the beam of Caitlin's smile & I wonder if what makes a
treasure, a treasure is the box you put it in. Called today — a video.
                Your face — bracketed and then soon   gone.

What do you keep in your quiet?

My stomach hurts
                and I can't sleep, not knowing if this heavies you.

Can you still pinch flightful things from the air with just your fingers (how)? How do
you soft this unsoaring? Take a fluttering thing from the still — a treasure
torn from its miracle sibling.

Tell me.   Am I as dark as a box beneath the bed?

Do you know what an us sounded like before you safed it? Buried somewhere
          without language.

I am certain
          I could look,   but
                    how can we talk about this
                                                            forever?

A Horse Problem

If you could do me a kindness and never make me
look at a painting of horses at sunset, again —
That would be worth all of the gratitude I am capable of.
I mean, *thank you*. Who knew
I/you could only take so many of/from the wealth of my palette/my heart &
what beauty I could carry/be carried by before my pockets turned out and
I began to/still stare so blankly at the proud muscle bathed in rose &
think it nothing of me?

Please.
Take the frame from me/me from it.

I have run too long stopping where I am told/to the edge but no further.
There is nothing more/more for *me* here —
just beyond where the marigold curls its lips I would rest/kiss,
if you let me kick dust up & go.

I court the fire as I do the yon
without ever knowing the
nail or the name
it hangs.

Sunset IV

Your smile soft, though I left
with little red crescents in my arms — I do not
think you meant them — I dream of the moons you trace into
your leg in comfort and the comfort they give me now. I remember
the way you rocked your head and yalped   a whale   a whale   a whale
at every blue bod yon & know you love the breathing mountain, how it bellows
as I do (& try not to) — floats on the horizon like a babe cradled in song and on the
days you do not speak this is how I divorce each jagged thing that means to sink me.

8/9/21

Again with the washing of hands, but
I am worried about the passings on.
Miracles, in real time, may seem a glimmer, but I suppose all collect dust.
Handprints, new or old, are handprints.
Months pass and tan my sheets.
Brooms lose their fingers in the floorboards

                                  & make work for later brooms.

In August we sweat for need of shade & in January for need of a clean sweater — yes.

I wish this were a loved one's wet
as I might honor that history with my tongue,
                 but these are a stranger's photos.
                          They gray me in ways I can't handle.
I change all the bulbs to see
the water run clear away.

I check the mirror to make sure I am unsalted
in the home you have built & share with me.

I'll shake your hand, nervous —
ready to tarnish the space with honor.

Re: The Jig of Life

I am hard as an urn
           am cracking every day —   ever full with ashes
           am what you put in me   am what is put into me
           am what I put in me   put in me
           am what I eat
Easter Sunday —   stuffing cloves of garlic & rosemary into the boar
Easter Sunday —   tin sheets in the pit
Easter Sunday —   shovel into the dry dirt
              wet burlap, wet burlap
                   all the hands at work or at work drinking
                   all eyes on the bits of door and shed turning charcoal
Come on, and let me live
              Come on, and let me live
I leave seeds to wake in jars at the window
              little life, what little life   can come back to me?
I press into the earth until my hands bleed

I just want a life where I can feed you
                             and feed me too
Which means
              I do   I do   just want   a life
                              Let me have it
                                   Jesus, Let me have it
                                        even if it breaks me

4/1/20

Every day
I grow all the more curious of
how much of me still goes
when all else suddenly stops
    (it seems).

Tonight I jog the block
'til I break a sweat   and halt.

Take note —
my breath grows longer
though my soles seem
to singe and thin
    (albeit slightly).

My boots are distinctly
giving it up   floor-ward
but I'm kinda   not.

This morning, I coughed hard
and promptly measured every last hair
on my head   goodness.

Where does the uncoiling live in the body?
I thought
I would've found the knot
by now, but I keep
waking

to a coal-hot discomfort
in my neck & ceaseless questions.

My throat harbors
some hard still-ing
& in these idle times I find it hard to ignore.

Something on the anvil of me keeps ringing
no matter how I go
    (or do not go).

I do not know.

I am just thankful
            to have something
                        to work through.
Oh, how I do.

SUNSET VII

I even let you touch my throat.
The way you scrunch your lips when your mind is
working comforts me when I give my head to your blade.
It is my trust that hurts me, its hard edges on every break . It is my
want that hurts me — the world to stop hurting you. You give and you
you give from the cup I fill and I fill and I fill and that is so beautiful, but I am
giving you my only neck. It's all I have to offer, and ironically I'd trade it for your life.

RE: HELLO EARTH

Crossing over the desert brow
                 spare ranges, sparse rivers
I see the red lights
                 south & how softly they wave their fingers

Who are all these places we call home?
                 Do all our roots have voices we can simply call or cut off?

The pecan tree coughs fruit
                 onto to the ground,
                    mockingbirds sing for the bounty
in my mind they dance iridescent, but they are black
in my mind the oranges always orange, but they are green
                 the roses — gone
                 the tree & viny terrace — gone
                 the dog — gone, resting infinite in the roses
                 the long, long table at Guadalajara ever shorter
                 illness chopping at the end like a mill, daily
Why did I go?   *Why did I go?*
                 In my mind I never left and that's the problem
But I'm not here   *But I'm not here*
for these rocky waters (in my mind) an endless ocean
for these rocky waters (in my mind) in the eye of a storm
                 (in my mind) is there anything I can offer
other than to tend the irrigation
                    to patch the roof
                    to pick the oranges
                    to offer my words

When I am home,
I offer my silly, silly words (ocean endless)
                 I offer my meager hours to share your table (ocean endless)
                 to receive your stories (ocean endless)
                 to get your advice on care for my chiles though the mulberries
                 blanketed with flies and rot months ago

Tell me —
                 tell me that one again
                    you were how old when you rode your first plane?
                    looking out over the fields of tomato
                your head in the hum, their red in the dirt
                    did they look like fireworks?

LIVING FOR NOW, QUEER FOR AS LONG AS WE CALL IT THAT

Walking the denim until the crotch blows out
fizzy water, saving half — light the match
last twelve dollars just for ambiance
somewhere else, early bus, early bus back
emerging February polishing
rosy 'round the cheeks and eyes watering
hey sorry — do you have lotion on you
do you have the space for me to tell you
never mind — french fries tiny fish & wine
tall can cliff bar tall can and cigarette
fire in the backyard, smokey jacket
if we can make these moments last for days
the living may live for that much longer
the days they will wash out but I'll linger

small tricks — it's all we can do
tend to our tiny candles
reach out our scrawny windows
mend our bodies, mind our breath
through the wet and windy March
catch the shift, crash on the couch
my friend it's been awhile
it's been a wild time, yeah
ya know — I need something green
I can't tell what's serving me
do I look that much better?
be honest what can be done
to try to stop the fading
I'll stay until I find out.

SUNSET VIII

From the train past Mystic
it is pink, tomato pink. This moment I can breathe
and it is such a gift to sit with you, before the empty city streets
(also a gift), so I ask what can be done, new friend? When what you do
does so much for others, how do you find rest ever (or this December) and
he asks What is there? What does one even do? & I promise friend, I am looking
for the answer for all of us lest we all spend our nights just simply catching our breath

RE: THE MORNING FOG

Woke in
            the grocery store.
                        Hands in the dried fruit
startle me   by my presence.

Mango slices —   avian egg red
                        12 dollars for a fistful— damn.
Hands red
            then pink
                        then olive.
Estuaries to patches of knuckle bristle —
fur in several sun colors.

I am certain   I look lost   in the mouth.
Agape with wanderlust
                        for the motive
                        for the morning.
Tuesday

I'll tell my father I
            came here for something
I wake fast-footed —
                        body peels out with my ghost
                                    on the roof, still.

Ah Christ, I even named the damn thing
                        cared for it
                        stole its gaze back from the mirror.
But damn   *damn*
                  this vacancy.
Damn me —   text back my brother.

I would feel so rich to be inhabited by a fool
or a loved one
    than to have paddled here.
                        No oar
                            nor understanding
                            of the river
                            or where the spirit rests
                            and what it looks up at
                            when it looks   not through me.

BEAVERS

I feel as if I should tell you that I have never yet, seen
a beaver in the wild —
but have, for sure seen plenty of things:
      Too many a shrub and quail
          Elk drunk at the waterfall
              Horses arrogant in the sun (with their four legs)
   So many a video of fruit bats gnawing on   fruit.
   So many dams made by clawed hands   or less clawed hands.

I however, unseen, still strong-arm the river
at the diaphragm in wanting — and choke.
Think I grow more confident in the frame I wake in —
Every rock & word shifts to coerce the spirit outside the vessel & up
the shore, pregnant, affirmed.
      I hope I am loud enough to beckon *help*
            as the water's edge keeps climbing.

I'm sorry, it is rude to think myself a river, more than animal.
I fear the space I take, knowing my gender is too wide and coursing.
I don't want to scare whatever gets swallowed by my shadow.
I've been swallowed,
        and have seen all not bashfully shrouded by my lashes —

Sometimes I burst in a partner's mouth & a dam breaks —
floods all my being &
I do not see it coming
      go warm as doubt drowning, but
          hear my name called to me over crashing timber, this time.

It is enough to keep safe until morning,
enough when my friends call me a Mother in earnest.
It is a truth with heavy hands, which laps at the levee without relent.
But *most times*   I cradle my stomach and do not feel a fertile shore.
Even in the rushing water.

I weep and search the mirror for a place to rescue my wanting —
wonder so often if all who love me must breathe water,
or just as unlikely, make a home in my body solely by their mouths
or clawed hands,
      or whatever raw will a wild thing has
to take shelter in impossible places.

I have not yet seen one for me in my wandering.
this being that treads stream and earth confident
without fear until just here in my room
through the eyes of another.

I've sought this force of nature —
& every minute knowing the deficit of
the sense to believe those close/in love without always seeing.
& it is enough of a miracle.
                        Oh, natural splendor
to hear your name from a loved one's
mouth,   breath,   begin to trust and well,

I suppose,   I could have just led with that.

SUNSET IX

This far out,   I can
never tell whether the sun rises or
sets — the answer (I know) is both, but I forget

NOTES

The structure of *Keep Your Little Lights Alive* and many of its poems are after Kate Bush's *Hounds of Love* album. The book, like the album, is split into two halves entitled *Re: Hounds of Love (A)* and *Re: The Ninth Wave (B)* with poems entitled "Re:___" taking their names directly from the songs they are after and appearing in the same sequence they do in the album.

The opening quote "Come on…" and poem title "Let Me Steal This Moment From You Now" come directly from the song "Running Up that Hill (A Deal with God)."

The opening quote for *Re: Hounds of Love (A)* "Tell me we…" is a direct quote from the song "Running Up That Hill (A Deal with God)."

"Re: Running Up that Hill (A Deal with God)" includes a partial quote from the song: "If I only could, I'd make a deal with God."

The title "Let's Exchange the Experience" is a quote from "Running Up that Hill (A Deal with God).

The title "It's in the Trees, It's Coming" is a quote from the sound clip at the beginning of the song "Hounds of Love." It is originally taken from the 1957 film *Night of the Demon*.

The earliest form of "Re: Hounds of Love II" is an erasure of the song "The Big Sky."

"Rabbit" opens with a quote from Paddy McAloon's song "Moving the River" off of Prefab Sprout's 1985 album *Steve McQueen*.

The title "Am I the Cat that Takes the Bird" is a quote from the song "Mother Stands for Comfort."

"Re: Cloudbusting" opens with a quote from Eric Dovigi's poem "Mr. Smith the Pirate Killer, Pt 1."

Re: The Ninth Wave (B) opens with the quote "We are of the going water…" which appears in the songs "Waking the Witch" and "Jig of Life" and was written and performed by John Carder Bush.

The line in "Re: Watching You Without Me," "Can you know the lengths to which I keep your little lights alive," is a reference to the line "We should make the night, but see your little lights alive" from "Waking the Witch."

The title "I Put this Moment, Here" is a quote from the song "Jig of Life."

The poem "Re: Hello Earth" takes the line "Why did I go" from the song "Hello Earth," and the line "but I'm not here" from the song "Watching You Without Me."

ACKNOWLEDGEMENTS

A Big, Infinite THANK YOU to *Write Bloody* for giving this collection a home! Thank you to Derrick Brown & Nikki Steele for your hard work and direction. Thank you to Wess Mongo Jolley for your profound work in polishing and focusing these poems — your thoughtful notes mean so much to me.

·

Thank you, my Gawd, *thank you* to the editors and staff of the following journals, in which poems (occasionally in earlier versions) from this collection first appeared:

Pigeon Pages: "Re: Running Up That Hill (A Deal with God)" and "Re: The Big Sky"

COUNTERCLOCK: "Re: Cloudbusting"

Voicemail Poems: "Beavers"

Drunk in a Midnight Choir: "Pull the Rail"

Maps for Teeth: "Anise (Cochitos)"

Queer.Archive.Work. (Urgency Reader Series): "I Know, in Some Ways, I Must be Answering for All the Times I Begged for More Time in my Kitchen" and "8/9/2021"

Red Clover Press: "Dress a" and "3/1/21"

·

Thank you to the Editors, Staff, and Collaborators who were so kind as to include me in the following projects:

Slamfind: "Small Things and All After Them (Daniel)"
and Mason Granger — when I think of what I miss about our community, I think of you foremost.

Game Over Books: "And Dream of Sheep"
a version of which appears as a Suit in the "I Wish I Wasn't Royalty: A Playable Chapbook" deck of cards. Thank you Josh Savory for your relentless dedication, and Catherine Weiss for your creative voice in all things — we are so lucky for you both.

Ours Poetica (in collaboration with the Poetry Foundation): "Re: Watching You Without Me"
A special shout out to Charlotte Abotsi who I cheer for daily. I wish you curated everything — like, in the world.

Daedelus (a performance for ACCUTE 2022): "Re: Cloudbusting"
Specifically the kind man behind the music — Alfred Darlington. Gratitude for the new friendship that fueled and inspired the last push towards this collection.

THANK YOU

To the Champions of my Heart:

Emil Eastman, Sam Rush, Jess Rizkallah, Levi Cain, Muggs Fogarty, Charlotte Abotsi, Wil Williams, Geoff Jackson, Gabbi Jue, Brenda Quintana, Adam Kelley, Nikko Fyfe, Zenaida Peterson, Sara Mae, and Ben Sohr. "Re: Waking the Witch" is for you, but none of these poems would have been possible without you.

To my Family:

Caitlin Maria, James Anthony, and Cassie Anne Quiñonez — for growing all the most glowing parts of my heart. I am so proud of the beautiful, kind people you are. Carolyn Lynch & Louis Quiñonez — for making me, your love, and all the tools you have given me for getting through this wild world. Maria & Manuel Quiñonez — for seeing and loving me. I am seeing and loving you, daily. Lisa Quiñonez & Colleen Lynch Bahle — for showing me how to keep art & joy close. Michelle, Steve, Sheila, Louie, Angie, Pat, Alex, Mannie, Terry, Dan, Anne, Mike, Kristen, Brian, and Kevin, Jim, and Marlene — thank you.

To the Shredders that Inspire me, Daily:

Porsha Olayiwola, George Abraham, Charissa Lucille, Emily Tatham, Torrin A. Greathouse, Devin Samuels, Astrid Drew, Chrysanthemum Tran, Devin Devine, Jane Gerber, Justice Ameer, Ally Ang, Rachel McKibbens, Clementine Von Radics, Joe Pera, Emmanuel Oppong-Yeboah, JR Mahung, Casey Belisle, Roz Raskin, EDT, Will Farrell, sam m-h, lids bday, olive, addie, Grace Ward, Tom Weyman, JB, Glenna Van Nostrand, Breanna Castro, Julia Claire Leveille, Kimberly Jarchow, Robbie Dunning, Jamie Rhode, Eric Dovigi, Andrew Ibrado, Tycho, Jules Zuckerberg, Nafis White, and Paul Soulellis. I am so grateful to love and carry you with me.

To the Angels Collective:

Jessa, Mary, Mimi W., Blue, Cath, Mimi C., Becki, Jeanine and Lilly. Oh my Gawd, love to love you. I wish to live in the worlds you create.

To Big Feeling, Glou, Bolt Coffee, and the Columbus Theatre:

These spaces mean so much to me.

To the Albums that Carried me Through the Making of this Book:

Lomelda — *Hannah*
Beverly Glenn-Copeland — *Keyboard Fantasies*
Dylan Henner — *The Invention of the Human*
Karima Walker — *Waking the Dreaming Body*
Nala Sinephro — *Space 1.8*
Felbm — *Elements of Nature*
Jeff Parker — *The New Breed*
Resavoir — *Resavoir*
Dezron Douglas, Brandee Younger — *Force Majeure*
The Handsome Family — *Milk & Scissors*
Carlos Niño, Miguel Atwood-Ferguson — *Chicago Waves*
Prefab Sprout — *Steven McQueen*
Alice Coltrane, Pharoah Sanders — *Journey in Satchidananda*
Alabaster DePlume — *To Cy & Lee: Instrumentals Vol. 1*
Green-House — *Six Songs for Invisible Gardens*
Fresh Pepper — *Fresh Pepper*

Y'all have kept my dreams alive & head on straight — to not acknowledge your part in this would be a deep shame. Thank you for all that you do and all I get to experience.

And, of course — to Kate Bush for *Hounds of Love*:

Thank you for making work that has grounded many of my favorite memories — the laughter, the dancing, long car rides, empty venues, wooden floors, rainy walks in my headphones, trying and failing to paint my nails, all of it. To be finishing this project four years after it started and hear your songs ever present on the radio feels like a spell I can't ignore.

Who really knows why and how our ripples turn into open windows for others, but it is an honor to sing from what these tracks have given me. Thank you, Forever.

JOHN-FRANCIS QUIÑONEZ (THEY/THEM) is a

Desert Flower & Current Resident of Providence, RI /
Queer Writer & Multimedia Artist /
Maker of ice creams & tamales /
House Manager of the Columbus Theatre /
Current Resident of the Queer.Archive.Work. project/

Find more of their work at: *www.johnfrancisquinonez.com*

IF YOU LIKE JOHN-FRANCIS QUIÑONEZ, JOHN-FRANCIS QUIÑONEZ LIKES...

Cut to Bloom
by Arhm Choi Wild

Floating Brilliant Gone
by Franny Choi

Lessons on Being Tender Headed
by Janae Johnson

This Way to the Sugar
by Hieu Minh Nguyen

In the Pockets of Small Gods
by Anis Mojgani

Write Bloody Publishing publishes and promotes great books of poetry every year.
We believe that poetry can change the world for the better. We are an independent press dedicated to
quality literature and book design, with an office
in Los Angeles, California.

We are grassroots, DIY, bootstrap believers. Pull up a good book and join the family. Support
independent authors, artists, and presses.

Want to know more about Write Bloody books, authors, and events?
Join our mailing list at

www.writebloody.com

WRITE BLOODY BOOKS

After the Witch Hunt — Megan Falley

Aim for the Head: An Anthology of Zombie Poetry — Rob Sturma, Editor

Allow The Light: The Lost Poems of Jack McCarthy — Jessica Lohafer, Editor

Amulet — Jason Bayani

Any Psalm You Want — Khary Jackson

Atrophy — Jackson Burgess

Birthday Girl with Possum — Brendan Constantine

The Bones Below — Sierra DeMulder

Born in the Year of the Butterfly Knife — Derrick C. Brown

Bouquet of Red Flags — Taylor Mali

Bring Down the Chandeliers — Tara Hardy

Ceremony for the Choking Ghost — Karen Finneyfrock

A Constellation of Half-Lives — Seema Reza

Counting Descent — Clint Smith

Courage: Daring Poems for Gutsy Girls — Karen Finneyfrock, Mindy Nettifee, & Rachel McKibbens, Editors

Cut to Bloom — Arhm Choi Wild

Dear Future Boyfriend — Cristin O'Keefe Aptowicz

Do Not Bring Him Water — Caitlin Scarano

Don't Smell the Floss — Matty Byloos

Drive Here and Devastate Me — Megan Falley

Drunks and Other Poems of Recovery — Jack McCarthy

The Elephant Engine High Dive Revival — Derrick C. Brown, Editor

Every Little Vanishing — Sheleen McElhinney

Everyone I Love Is a Stranger to Someone — Annelyse Gelman

Everything Is Everything — Cristin O'Keefe Aptowicz

Favorite Daughter — Nancy Huang

The Feather Room — Anis Mojgani

Floating, Brilliant, Gone — Franny Choi

Glitter in the Blood: A Poet's Manifesto for Better, Braver Writing — Mindy Nettifee

Gold That Frames the Mirror — Brandon Melendez

The Heart of a Comet — Pages D. Matam

CPSIA information can be obtained
at www.ICGtesting.com
Printed in the USA
BVHW051005211022
649935BV00003B/15